Almost an Addict

Bill Vancil

Copyright 2016
William D. Vancil

All rights reserved.

ISBN 978-1-365-39807-0

Foreword
by Dr. Mark Moskowitz

This is an enjoyable, matter-of-fact, and intimate narrative of one man's dependency with the opiate, oxycodone. It purposefully refers to the important differences between physical dependency and addiction. The latter is a pathological drug-seeking behavior leading to dysfunction (job/marriage loss) and even crime. People will steal; do almost anything to get the drug. And it is not just to relieve pain – it is to get high, and this is the prime distinction between an addict, and someone who is physically dependent on opioids. You can de-tox an addict, but his pathology most often leads him back to the drug. The word, "addict "has a sleazy, felon-like association.

Physical dependency was Bill Vancil's problem. He was not an addict. However, his dependency could have led to addiction, had he not followed his doctors' prescribed regimen. Bill became physically dependent on opioids not due to some character weakness or malpractice on the part of the doctors. Almost an Addict is an easy-to-read, lay-it-on-the-line story that will likely prove valuable to others who are physically dependent on opioids.

Mark J Moskowitz, MD
Diplomate, American Board of Internal Medicine,
Medical Oncology, and Hospice/Palliative Care
Manchester, United Kingdom

Prologue

It was two-thirty in the morning. I could hear them approaching, quietly moving down the darkened corridor, bent on torturing me. They bolted into my room and ungraciously flipped me over as if I were a rack of ribs on the grill. It was the dreaded night shift nurses. They showed up every night, shortly after their roller derby practice, I suspected. "Gentle," I would tell them, "Be gentle. Go easy. Slower. C'mon, that hurt!" They never listened.

"Sorry, Mr. Vancil, you don't want to get bed sores; you have to keep turning," they would tell me. "And, it's time for your pain medication. Take these, and we'll leave you alone to go back to sleep."

"Back to sleep?" I thought, "To what end? So another nurse can come in and draw some blood or check my catheter?" I reached for the Styrofoam glass of tepid water on the nightstand. Two more pills down the hatch. I had just had a liver transplant. The painkillers were a welcomed relief. Eventually, after three and a half months in the hospital, I was able to go home, taking with me a new liver, the challenge of learning to walk again, and a dependency on the opiate oxycodone. I continued to take this deviously comforting, potentially deadly opiate for six years, under the pretense that it was for "chronic pain relief." The fourteen-inch scar across my abdomen was my ticket to getting away with this illusory excuse.

My primary physician dutifully wrote prescriptions month after month. He well knew what I was up against, but he never used the word "addiction" or "dependency." But, he knew.

Chapter 1 – MELD Score

It was not my intention to become dependent on oxycodone. In late December 2009, I entered Meriter Hospital in Madison, Wisconsin for a seemingly routine surgery to repair an inguinal hernia. The surgery went well. I had not expected to be in the hospital for more than a day or two; generally, hernia surgery is not a big deal. While I was in recovery, nurses offered painkillers but I declined, explaining that I had never liked taking them. Pain killers tended to do weird things to me, cause goofy dreams. Two days, and still in recovery, the doctors told me that my liver functions, which had been troublesome prior to the hernia procedure, were getting worse and I would have to remain for observation. They sounded concerned. I became such, as well.

During the next few days, the problem worsened greatly. My ankles were swollen to twice-normal size, my skin had a yellowish tint, and my MELD score was increasing rapidly. (The Model for End-Stage Liver Disease, MELD, is a measure of mortality risk in patients with liver disease. It is used to measure how urgent the need for transplant. The range is from six (less ill) to 40 (gravely ill.) Okay, things were getting serious. Somehow, the term, "end stage" had an ominous ring to me. I started to accept the inevitable. I would need a new liver. Within a couple more days, things got even worse; my MELD score was somewhere *above* 40 - in technical terms used by the doctors, "off the charts."

Chapter 2 – Off to the Transplant Clinic

Wisconsin winters can be torturous. The temperature was eight degrees in the bowels of the parking garage at Meriter Hospital. The smell of exhaust fumes drifted across the concrete floor as the attendants rolled my gurney toward the waiting ambulance. I was on my way to the Transplant Clinic at the University of Wisconsin Hospitals and Clinics. Upon arriving, there was a place waiting for me in the Intensive Care Unit. Doctors gave me a blood transfusion, some other trauma center procedures; and I remained there several days.

Finally, I stabilized enough to move to a private room. There I would wait until, and if, a new liver became available. My room was not far from the helicopter-landing pad, close enough that I could hear the thrumming of the blades whenever one landed. Each time, I would wonder if it had my liver aboard.

While I awaited a new liver, nurses and doctors provided treatment to keep me stable, comfortable, and best of all, alive. I continued to resist taking pain medication. It had never crossed my mind that I could become dependent. I had not studied the subject, so I was unaware that millions of people become dependent, even addicted to pain medications, and many die from overdoses.

Nurses would ask me, "Would you like some pain medication, Mr. Vancil?" Up until the time of my transplant surgery, my response was typically, "No thank you, and call me Bill." Repeatedly I would hear, "Do you need some pain meds, Bill?" They were only trying to keep me comfortable. Some of the nurses may have been aware of the risk of dependency, but never mentioned it, and in my situation, it was a moot point.

I was fortunate to be at the University of Wisconsin Transplant Clinic. It is one of the best in the world. As of 2014, they had performed more than 2,000 liver transplants, 9,000 kidney transplants, and well over 700 heart transplants. They recognized the seriousness of my situation and placed me on a waiting list of patients in dire need of a donor liver. In the meantime, while I waited. I listened for the helicopters landing, watched the NFL Playoffs including the peculiarity of Bret Favre quarterbacking the Minnesota Vikings, and had my attorneys visit me to go over my last will and testament. To me, that smacked of a lack of optimism, but seemed a necessary exercise. It took a while, lawyers charge by the hour you know, and I recall telling them, "Let's wrap this up. I am tired of talking about dying. I want to talk about living." They left, several hundreds of dollars later, and I felt good that we had brought my will up-to-date. It was as good a time as any to do it.

Chapter 3 – At Last, the Helicopter

When the doctors came into my room and told me it was time to get on with the surgery, I felt only relief – no fear. I could not have been more prepared. I had complete confidence in the team of doctors, and I had been receiving strong support from my family and friends. I remember having a nervous smile on my face as a crew of doctors and nurses rolled me down the chilled hallway into the operating room. I was wrapped only in a clean white sheet, and my positive attitude.

As it turned out, there were actually *two* surgeries. The chief surgeon, Dr. Luis Fernandez, had deemed the first liver he installed to be unacceptable, and he put me on another priority list. This time I was in the number one position on a list that covered a five state area. It took just a few days for another liver to become available. Somehow, they kept me alive in the interim, though I did not regain consciousness until after the second surgery.

During my time in the operating room, while under a jumbo dose of anesthesia, I experienced a series of bizarre, mostly terrifying dreams. In one of these mini nightmares, vandals had ravaged my home, and across the street, a school bus was blowing up. At one point, I was aboard a speeding commuter train, and zipped past a brick wall with a graffiti message that read, "Your dad is dead." When the train stopped to pick up more people, a swarm of chattering little beasty creatures, which appeared to be half bird, half lizard, invaded it.

Another dream had me managing a drive-in theater in Hawaii, which featured live daredevils wearing ballerina skirts, sliding down a thin wire from the top of the theater screen. In another hideous dream, doctors placed a wire under the skin of my face, attached it to a bowling ball, placed the ball on my head, and knocked it off with a golf club. Horror film producer Wes Craven could not have come up with anything as scary.

When the exhaustive, senseless dreams finally ended, I began to awaken, seeing blurred images emerging through the fog, the first thing I heard, from across the room, was someone saying that I had *two* transplants. I started asking everyone who passed by, "Did I have two transplants?" Not until Dr. Fernandez himself told me, was I convinced. I had only signed up for one. He explained, "The first was not a good liver. It would not have served you well. So we got another…and it is a good one." He repeated, "It is a *really* good one."

Now the long road to recovery would begin and would take many weeks. The physical and occupational therapy would start soon in the hospital and would continue at home, assuming I would eventually make it home. However, for the moment, I was still bed-ridden with countless tubes running in and out of my body. I needed assistance doing everything, except complaining about the constant and intense pain. This is about the time I changed my mind about taking pain medications. A fourteen-inch incision across your belly, sealed by dozens of metal staples, and a collection of tubes transporting fluids in and out of your body, and nurses flipping you over in the night, will do that.

Chapter 4 – Tender Loving Care

I had received my new liver on February 10, 2010. For the next few weeks, my home was the TLC unit at UW Hospital. At first glance, TLC would suggest Tender Loving Care; on that they delivered, but the real meaning of TLC is Trauma and Life Support Center. The majority of patients admitted to TLC are critically ill patients who require aggressive intervention, patients who have undergone aortic aneurysm repair, extensive facial reconstruction, and liver transplantation as well as those who have experienced multi-system failure. In other words, you have to be in bad shape to get in to the TLC. I could not have been in a better place. During my stay, I underwent countless procedures - many were intrusive and painful. I had so many tubes hooked up to my body; I looked an octopus eating spaghetti. Thankfully, I had the benefit of pain pills. Virtually every four hours a nurse would ask if I needed pain medication. More often than not, I seriously *did* need it. Becoming acquainted with the painkiller oxycodone, I learned to appreciate the comfort it could provide. I did not realize it, but I was developing a dependency, and at that point probably did not care.

"Time for your pain medicine, okay?" chirped one of the tender, loving, caring nurses, "Do you want one or two?"

"Two, please," I always responded, hoping the next four hours would pass quickly.

Chapter 5 – Therapy, and More Therapy

During the latter part of February and the month of March, 2010, I spent my time lying in my hospital bed refusing to eat most of the hospital food, having visitors, taking phone calls from friends, and doing both physical and occupational therapy. It was strenuous, learning to walk and perform everyday tasks again. There was a joy and sense of accomplishment when I piloted an aluminum walker twelve feet down the hospital corridor. I worked out, best I could, on all kinds of exercise equipment. And, when the physical therapist would come to take me for my twice-daily workouts, he or she would often say, "It might be easier today, if you take your pain meds before we start." Sure, why not? Easier is good.

The occupational therapy was different, and not as stressful, nor as painful. It was easy, putting little blocks in little holes and stacking things up. The physical therapists were working toward making it possible for me to leave the hospital and continue the physical therapy at home; eventually leading to my doing all the normal things I did before my surgery. I can say proudly and thankfully that the long process worked. Today, I walk at least a mile every day; I can swim, play golf, drive the car, and dig holes in the hard Arizona soil to plant stuff.

"You know they won't let you out of here until you are eating properly," Mr. Vancil. 'We are keeping track of the calories. Did you take your pain pills?" Acknowledging my obligatory tilted nod, the nurse picked up the tray full of mostly uneaten hospital food, and disappeared into the well-lit corridor. Automatically, I picked up the two little white pills and washed them down with a gulp of Seven-Up, long since gone flat.

After a while in the hospital, it seemed there was no day or night. It was common to wake up from a nap at five o'clock in the afternoon, as the glow of twilight snuck through the window, and believe it was morning. Today, it is hard to fathom that I was in the hospital for well over one hundred days…or were they nights? Wisconsin winters were always tough to deal with. This winter was without doubt the toughest ever for me, even though I never donned a parka or even a stocking cap. I remember looking out the hospital room window as snow fell and thinking, "I'd rather be shoveling snow."

Chapter 6 – Time to Go Home

The staff of doctors, therapists, and nutritionists had decided on a date for me to leave the hospital, April 16, 2010. A nurse wrote it in large lettering on a white board in my room. We talked of my possibly going to a rehabilitation center, a "half-way house," prior to returning to my home. I found none of the places we considered acceptable, and asked the doctors to just let me go home. I knew I could continue the rehab on my own, with help from the visiting therapists whom they said would come and help. Done deal. I would go directly home on April 16th. I did eat enough to raise my calorie count sufficiently for them to discharge me. I would take home a new liver, a deep appreciation for the doctors and nurses, and a dependency for the opiate, oxycodone.

Thus, the routine began. Rehab continued at home with visits by both the physical and occupational therapists. Frankly, their visits became a bit of an annoyance after a fashion. The simple exercises they had me do were things I was doing on my own anyway. I was taking so many different drugs, including insulin because I had temporarily become diabetic, that the university pharmacy was shipping all the meds to me on a weekly basis. The shipment included oxycodone. Later, after I was back on my feet, and eventually able to drive, the routine changed. I would pick up my meds at the hospital; but for my oxycodone, I was required to get a new prescription each time, there were no "refills."

Every month, Dr. Kilpatrick would write a thirty-day prescription, I would drive to downtown Madison and pick it up, have it filled at the pharmacy, and continue taking two five-milligram tablets of oxycodone three times a day, every day. Upon moving from Madison to Arizona in 2013, my new primary physician, Dr. Gortner, picked up where Dr. Kilpatrick had left off, writing my monthly prescriptions. He, too, knew of my dependency, he might have been the first to use the word in my presence. Oxycodone was in my system continuously, at a rate of 30 milligrams per day, my body had become enamored with the opiate, and would raise a trembling red flag if I did not faithfully swallow the pills as prescribed.

While I had trouble confessing, even to myself, that I had a dependency, I was smart enough to know that the dosage must be carefully controlled, for two reasons: to make sure the doctor's orders were followed, and to not run out before the next prescription. I kept my intake under strict control for more than six years. Finally, I admitted that I had a dependency, and decided that, although I had managed it well and faced no serious health crisis, it had become a terrible inconvenience. Furthermore, for what I was paying each month for the oxycodone, I could play an extra round of golf each month, or have a Sonoran hot dog once a week.

Chapter 7 – Ending the Dependency

In August 2016, I decided that I'd had enough of this so-called friend, oxycodone. I had studied the subject and I knew that the only way to end such a relationship would be to do it gradually. Oxycodone shouted out, "Let me down easy." That was my plan; take it slowly. Several years after my surgery, having long recovered my ability to walk and do normal activities, I still relied on my friend oxycodone to maintain a normal level of physical comfort. Yet, at that point, it had still not entered my mind that my body had become dependent upon the drug. I was just following doctor's orders. I still lived in Madison and Dr. Kilpatrick, who wrote my prescriptions, never used the term dependency or addiction, but he knew. He knew well before I did. Later, when I moved to Arizona, Dr. Kilpatrick gave me a letter to take along, recommending to any new doctor that I continue the oxycodone regimen. He told me, "If you have trouble getting prescriptions once you are there in Arizona, call me." He knew.

By now, you can see there is a big difference between dependency and addiction. One can be addicted to many things – not just prescription drugs. Cigarettes come to mind, and alcohol. In casual terms, one can also be "addicted" to Dr. Pepper, television, gummy bears, social media, chocolate, and working out. Although, I have never heard of anyone holding up a convenience store to get gummy bears. The word "addict", in serious discussion, is most often associated with the word "drug." As a kid, I developed an image of the typical drug addict. It was some bum sitting on the curb, unshaven, slouched over, with his battered shoes in the gutter. Later in life, I learned that people dependent upon prescription drugs, who take them over long periods under the guise of "chronic pain relief", are, in fact, running the risk of becoming an addict.

There are thousands, perhaps millions, of others in a similar situation. You cannot tell by looking at the insurance guy in the suit and tie, who hurt his back playing softball, that he is dependent. You cannot tell by looking at the checkout lady at the supermarket, who had knee surgery two years ago, that she is drug dependent. They are everywhere. Some maintain a level of drug-supported normalcy for many years. Others progress from basic pain killing meds to street drugs and deadly combinations. In my case, before I became acquainted with the term, dependency, I referred to myself as having a "controlled addiction." I think it was a fairly accurate description, using two words where one would suffice.

Chapter 8 – Setting a Plan

Withdrawal from oxycodone is easier said than done. Withdrawing from any opiate is a difficult procedure. Having decided to end my affair with oxycodone, I must now decide how to go about it. I concluded there are several ways, three in particular.

1)   Seek professional help from an established rehabilitation center, as either an inpatient or outpatient.

2) Do it yourself at home, under close supervision of a doctor or other qualified professional..

3) Do it yourself at home, with minimal supervision, supported by your own research, and self-discipline.

I chose a slight variation on number three. I started my withdrawal, and several days in, I discussed my plan with my primary physician, Dr. Gortner. He assured me I was on the right track. I promised to keep him posted on my progress. Here is why I decided to end my dependency in this manner:

A) I have self-regulated my oxycodone intake from the beginning. I have never strayed from the original prescription, never raised the dosage. This required a high degree of self-discipline.

B) Although I went to college, the skills, which have benefitted me most, are those, which have been self-taught. I do my homework. I am good at figuring things out. I am not known as a quitter. (Except for when I quit smoking more than a dozen years ago.)

My goal in writing this book, is to help others who may be in a similar situation. Some may be reluctant to check in to a rehab center, or involve a doctor, and may want to follow my lead. If it does not work going alone, the other options are still out there. Keep in mind, I am not a medical professional. I offer this account of my own experience for what it is - a plan that worked for me. Every situation is different. What worked for me may or may not work for somebody else. The type of opiate, the dosage strength, and frequency, length of time the person has been dependent, and mental attitude can all make the road to being opiate-free a path never before followed. Having said that, I will proceed to tell why and how I ended my affair with oxycodone.

Chapter 9 – Making Life Simpler

It took a lot of soul searching to commit to ending my dependency of more than six years. Oxycodone never got me in trouble, and I never had a desire to meet any of the other members of the opiate family, such as Demerol, methadone, hydrocodone, morphine, or heroin. Then why kick a sleeping dog? Oxycodone and I seemed to be getting along nicely. The reason to stop was simple. It just got to be too much of an inconvenience. I was no longer taking oxycodone to feel better, but rather just to feel normal - to not feel bad. It was necessary to pick up prescriptions in person at the doctor's office, and show identification at the pharmacy. Taking a medication, three times a day, over a long period, gets to be a bore. It was much busy work, with little redeeming value.

In mid-summer, 2016, when my primary physician, Dr. Gortner announced that he would be retiring he sent a brief note to all his patients stating that, after his retirement date, he would no longer be able to write prescriptions. I was already aware that my liver doctor, and other doctors I had seen were not willing to prescribe oxycodone. Talk of epidemic was all over the news channels, and pressure was mounting among lawmakers to make it more difficult for doctors to prescribe opiates. While I was fairly certain I could find a doctor to write the prescriptions, I thought, "Is this really worth the hassle?"

In addition to having to locate a willing prescription provider, there would be the continuing matter of logistics. Oxycodone is a controlled substance. There are tight restrictions on its distribution. Refills are not allowed; each prescription is a new one. It is a bad thing to lose a prescription. Do that and a replacement prescription is impossible to acquire. There is a form you must sign stating that you will only use your designated pharmacy, and that you will not share the drugs with anyone. You must also agree to a urine test if requested. The reason for the test is to make sure you ARE taking the meds and not sharing, stockpiling, or selling them. I never had to do that urine test. I always took my medicine. They knew.

Pharmacies have their regulations as well, if you have a series of monthly prescriptions you cannot fill one until the previous one is with a couple of days of running out. They will ask for ID every time as well. The other inconvenience is just the day-to-day routine of taking the oxycodone the prescribed number of times. Therefore, my decision to break up with my opiate friend was because it was an inconvenience. An untested concern was whether, after Dr. Gortner's retirement, I would be able to find a physician willing to prescribe oxycodone. I chose not to begin that search. Let the devil take tomorrow; let the question go unanswered.

Chapter 10 – Slow and Easy

Quitting a dependency to anything, must begin with making a firm commitment. After first assuring myself that I would see this through, I told several people close to me what I was doing It is imperative to have other people aware of your determination. It is important to choose persons whom you would not want to disappoint. Set yourself up to be embarrassed…and then do not let it happen. There you have the number one requirement to ending a dependency a firm, unbreakable commitment.

As I have stressed, there is only one way to end a relationship with oxycodone. Slowly and deliberately. You must taper off the dosage, reducing little by little, over time. One should not be in a hurry to end the relationship because oxycodone will not go away without a struggle. It is not a simple matter of letting the oxycodone work its way out of your system, or allowing it to leave through sweating and urinating. Oxycodone, over an extended period, causes physical changes within your brain. As you reduce the intake of the drug, the brain slowly returns to its intended condition (Notice I did not use the word "normal." Who has a normal brain?)

What I am going to document in the next chapter is the schedule I followed in reducing the dosage of oxycodone. I cannot claim it will work for anyone else, but it worked for me. There is more to this process than just determinedly following a schedule, and we will address that in another upcoming chapter.

Chapter 11 – Setting a Schedule

"I'm going to stop oxycodone, Dr. Gortner," I said, as he entered the exam room, preceded by a polite knock on the door, as doctors do. "In fact I've already started reducing the dosage." He was impressed, and supportive. I went over my plan and he thought it looked good.

Below is the schedule I followed. If someone else uses this as a guideline, I would caution that each case is different. Depending on the length of the dependency, the dosage, the willpower possessed by the patient, a plan different from mine may be appropriate.

For over six years, I had taken 30 milligrams of oxycodone every day. Usually, two tablets three times a day. Sometimes I spread the doses over the day differently, but total per day was always thirty. Here is the eight-week plan I created and followed:

Week 1 - 20 mg per day (one 5 mg tablet, 4 times a day)
Week 2 - 15 mg per day (one 5 mg tablet, 3 times a day)
Week 3 - 12..5 mg per day (1/2 tablet, 5 times a day)
Week 4 - 10 mg per day (1/2 tablet, 4 times a day)
Week 5 - 7.5 mg per day (1/2 tablet 3 times a day)
Week 6 - 5.0 mg per day (1/2 tablet twice a day)
Week 7 thru week 9 - 2.5 to 5 mg per day (1/2 tablet, once or twice a day, not to exceed 5 mg per day.)

Week 10 and beyond - Try to stay without taking any oxycodone. Allow yourself a safety net of ½ tablet each day, only when absolutely necessary. When you have gone a full 24 hours without any oxycodone, do not assume you are home free. You have reached what I call Ground Zero. Your daily intake of the opiate is now zero. The trick now is to stay at Ground Zero for seven consecutive days. Your daily intake is none. However, *do not consider yourself a failure* if you go two or three days, and find that you just have to take half a tablet. The important thing is that you NOT take a *larger* dose, and to realize that, having given in out of necessity, you are now back at Ground Zero, day one of what we are trying to stretch into seven consecutive days. Back up and start again each time this happens. Again, it does not mean you've failed, it just means you must return to the starting line. In the military, they call it being "recycled." Stay in your lane, stay determined, and you will get to the finish line.

If you are in the same situation as I was regarding the amount of oxycodone you have been taking (30 mg per day), the minimum time spent in withdrawal should be about nine to ten weeks. If you have enough five milligram tablets to extend the withdrawal to a longer period, it could make the process go a bit easier.

If you have been taking twice as much or more than I, then use percentages based on the above plan, decreasing by the same percentages. As an example, my first week's reduction was 30 mg to 20 mg. If you were taking 60 mg then reduce to 40 the first week, and so on.

Important: My plan, which we just explained, involved taking oxycodone only. If you have been taking an opiate different from oxycodone, especially stronger opiates such as heroin, see a medical professional for help with the plan. One plan does not fit all.

Chapter 12 – It's All in Your Head

Withdrawal from oxycodone or any opiate is not easy, it is right up there with quitting smoking and quitting alcohol. Making a commitment and setting an incremental timeframe are two things relatively easy to do. However, those things are just the start. Staying the course, getting it done, ending the dependency may not be quite so simple. In this chapter, we explore some of the real and possible pitfalls, detours, and frustrations that occur during withdrawal and how to deal with them.

Your body will not be happy about this - including your brain. It has not only experienced oxycodone coming into your body via little white pills, and leaving via sweating and urination, your brain has physically changed because of the long-term medication.

While you and your brain are moving through this metamorphosis, there will be times of stress. There will be times you question your decision to end the dependency. There will moments when it seems chains couldn't keep you from twisting the top of that little white bottle. These are the times you must be strong. While going through the withdrawal, I had to devise some mind games to take my thoughts away from the yearnings my body was shouting out. It is impossible to accomplish withdrawal by lying around thinking about it. One of the best ways I have found, to stay the course, is to keep busy. Remember, this is about your brain getting a re-boot, a correction. It takes time and determination, and sometimes distraction. During my withdrawal, I tried to find as many ways as I could to keep busy.

One project of sorts was I had been dieting. Being fifteen pounds lighter and realizing that dieting and opiate withdrawal do not get along very well, I allowed the diet to sacrifice a bit to serve the greater goal. Healthy snacking became one of my distractions. During the process, I only gained back three or four pounds.

I bought a keyboard a couple of years ago. The kind on which you play music, not the kind that sits near the computer. I started learning new songs, mostly old country standards and Fifties hits, because they are easier to play, usually only three or four chords. By the time I had completed the withdrawal, I learned to play nearly a dozen new songs – and memorized the lyrics to over half of them. This was a fun distraction. Don't watch for me on any television talent shows, however.

I launched a landscape project, adding some low voltage lighting and decorative stones to our backyard area. Summertime is Arizona is a hot time to do this, but I did it in spurts, early morning mostly when it was cooler; and the desert-like backyard now looks great..

The lease was up on my car, so I was able to treat myself to a new car. For any guy, that is a cool distraction, getting new wheels. I thought of excuses to drive places just to get behind the wheel and enjoy the imitation leather new car smell and the rattle-free ride.

If you consider watching television as keeping busy, then pick programs that keep you interested and involved, instead of a dull show from which it is easy to drift off mentally. Go to the grocery store without a list. Roam the store looking for healthy treats. Talk to the person behind the butcher counter. Buy some cake mix and bake a three-layer cake. Invent a recipe for chili. Plant a flower. Take up acrylic painting or photography.

Check out some of the video games available for your computer, TV, smart phone or iPad. My favorites are Leo's Fortune, Plants and Zombies, Ticket to Ride, and best game ever, Monument. Consider learning a second language. There is a terrific free app for your smart phone or tablet, called Duolingo. Esto es muy bueno.

Chapter 13 – Rough Ride Ending

Pausing for a brief summary and reminder, there are now three elements of importance when doing through withdrawal.

1) Commitment (including telling others)
2) Making a plan (as detailed as possible)
3) Keeping busy (don't lie down on this)

At every plateau that I reached as I moved through my withdrawal plan, I felt good about my progress. "Yes! I'm down to five tablets a day instead of six." The crowd went wild. Then, same thing when I reduced the dosage again, to four a day. When I reached three a day things got a bit tougher. I would get a bit shaky, sweat more at night, and a condition I have had since I was a kid, restless leg syndrome (RLS), would make its presence known, especially at bedtime. Dr. Gortner prescribed a medicine called rOPINIRole, clearly named by someone with a slim grasp on capitalization. This drug is used to treat RLS, but just as one must taper off oxycodone, one must "taper on" to rOPINIRole. You can see what was happening. Tapering off one drug, and tapering on to another, it became a puzzle as to which of the two drugs might be helping how I felt.

As these two drugs crossed paths, I had some troublesome nights. In the wee hours, my RLS would act up. I could not be sure if it was because the new drug, taken prior to bedtime, had worn off, or it was a symptom of my oxycodone withdrawal? It did not take long for me to acquire a distaste for rOPINIRole. It left me with a groggy, hangover type feeling toward the early hours of the morning. It also created an extremely dry mouth. I decided to taper back off the rOPINIRole, take a minimal dose and work on other ways to deal with RLS.

I was now down to just one to one-and-a-half tablets of oxycodone per day (5-7.5 mg) I was approaching what I came to call "Ice Station Zero (Zero for short)" where intake is reduced to NO oxycodone. However, I was not there yet. The closer one gets to Zero, more withdrawal symptoms occur, and they are more pronounced. According to the website recovery.org, "Oxycodone withdrawal often includes uncomfortable physical and mental symptoms that progress in intensity and may persist for as many as seven days (ed. after complete discontinuance.) Symptoms can include: Nausea and vomiting, diarrhea, abdominal cramps, hot and cold sweats, runny nose, fatigue, frequent yawning, muscle aches, insomnia, irritability, and anxiety."

Because I chose to withdraw from my dependence slowly, during the course of withdrawal, I did not experience all of those symptoms; there was some nighttime sweating, muscle aches and modest cramps, and fatigue. However, the aches and fatigue may have been the result of other things, including my dance partner, RLS, and perhaps just getting older. As I experienced these discomforts during the slow reduction in dosage, I was determinedly creeping closer and closer to Zero and beyond. (I continue to capitalize Zero because I considered it a point of reference, a place in time from which I would move further along.)

I thought I had reached Zero when, for the first time, I went over twenty-four hours without taking any oxycodone. It was actually more like thirty hours. My first full night past Zero, was spent tossing, turning, wondering if I should have stuck with the oPINIRole, doing some moaning and groaning, fighting a horrible aching in my legs and some in my shoulders. Hard as I tried, my body countermanded the objections swirling through my brain. I had no choice but to take a half tablet of oxycodone. It is important to note, that I did not feel as though I had failed. Sometimes you must take a step backwards to move a step forward. The key for me was to be careful not to take *too big* a step backwards. At that moment, I told myself that, during this process, I would not feel guilty if I occasionally deviated from the plan. I also pledged to never take more than a minimal dosage (one half to one tablet – 2.5 to 5 mg), and only when it seemed unavoidably necessary. I was beginning to realize that the early stages of withdrawal, such as when I dropped the dosage from 30 mg per day to 20 mg per day, are relatively easy. However, coming down the home stretch was far more difficult. Zero is a difficult place to reach, not a comfortable place to be, and a hard place to settle down. I began wondering how many times I might move in and out of this place. Going without oxycodone gradually became more comfortable.

It was just a couple of weeks more and I had leveled off at this place I called Ice Station Zero. With the help of another doctor (my primary doc retired during this whole process) we came up with a different plan to curtail the restless leg syndrome. With that now under control, it became easier to diminish the reliance on oxycodone. Finally, I was moving forward and began to appreciate the fact that I had improved my quality of life. Ice Station Zero was still in my rearview mirror, but getting further away every day. It had been an interesting six-year ride. As I said in the early chapters of this book, the dependency to oxycodone became more of an inconvenience than anything else. I had not strayed from the prescription details, never took the opiate recreationally, never thought of trying any other stronger opiates. While I had a very real dependency, at no time did I feel as though I was addicted. But, unknowingly, I was…*almost* an addict.

Conclusion – Short Book, One Purpose

By design, this is a short book. Its purpose is to tell the story of one man, me, who became dependent upon a prescription drug, and how he broke the dependency. That's all. I did not want to load up the story with a bunch of statistics, or accounts of other persons' stories, just in order to make a longer book. It is well known that "results may vary." Every case is different. If someone simply cannot do a withdrawal plan such as the personal plan I followed, they should not be considered a failure. There are other options available.

Under a doctor's supervision, sometimes a prescription drug called Suboxone is used to treat withdrawal. Suboxone is a combination of buprenorphine and naloxone; it is intended to provide relief from oxycodone withdrawal symptoms without the "high" of oxycodone. It is used during detox to alleviate the discomfort of withdrawal and reduce cravings. I cannot endorse it, because I have not used it. On the Internet, you will find a wide variety of other programs, plans, supplements, and places to go for treatment. Be sure to examine the credibility of any website visited to make sure they are honest and trustworthy. On the internet, one link can lead to another, so be cautious.

Remember, there is a big difference between dependency and addiction. Do not let one lead to the other. It is not easy to end a dependency. However, it is far more difficult to end an addiction, and sometimes an addiction can, sadly, end itself.

About the Author

Bill Vancil grew up the small town of Kewanee, Illinois. He attended Illinois Wesleyan University and Augustana College. For over thirty years, he lived in Madison, Wisconsin. Following a long career at Mid-West Family Broadcasting, as an announcer, program director, and vice-president/general manager, he was inducted into the Wisconsin Broadcasters Association Hall of Fame. He now lives in Marana, Arizona, where he is self-employed as a graphic designer and freelance writer.

In 2004, Bill received treatment for prostate cancer at Loma Linda University Proton Treatment Center. His first book was about this journey. "Don't Fear the Big Dogs" was published in 2005. Bill was featured in twenty-five Barnes & Noble book-signing events around the country. He appeared on more than seventy radio and television interviews discussing the book, one of the first books to incorporate facts about proton radiation treatment.

Appointed to the International Advisory Council of Loma Linda's Proton Center, Bill served in that capacity for ten years. Bill Vancil has visited every state in the union, except Alaska, and has toured over fifteen foreign countries. He is an accomplished graphic designer, painter, and photographer. In 2009, he published a children's book, "Roy and Kitty." In December of that year, Bill was admitted to the hospital where he spent over three months, undergoing two liver transplants and weeks of rehabilitation. During that hospital stay, he acquired a dependency upon oxycodone

Made in United States
North Haven, CT
11 April 2024